Nothing Definite Yeti

Nothing Definite Yeti

Richard Stevenson

Illustrations by Gail Shepley

Ekstasis  Editions

Canadian Cataloguing in Publication Data

Stevenson, Richard
    Nothing definite yeti.

    Poems
    Includes bibiographical references.
    ISBN 1-896860-50-4

    I. Shepley, Gail II. Title.
    Ps8587.T479N67   1999   C811'.54   C99-911148-5
    PR9199.3.S78728N67   1999

Acknowledgements:
Some of the poems in this collection, a sequel to Why Were All The Werewolves Men?
(Thistledown Press, 1994), have previously appeared or been accepted for issues of the
following anthologies, journals, electronic, city, and small magazines:
    All Mixed Up Writer's E-zine, Ariel: A Review of International English Lit-
erature (Postcolonial/ Postindependence Perspective: Children's and Young Adult
Literature issue), Canadian Author, The Canadian Anthology of Modern Verse For
Children (Ed. by I.B. Iskov — in manuscript), Chameleon (Department of Creative
Writing, U.B.C., Vancouver), Distant Horizons, Dream Forge, Eternity, Freefall (Fif-
teenth Anniversary Issue), Lethbridge Living, Lost Magazine, On Spec, Orphic
Chronicle, Porcerpine Press, Power Animal, Senary (Falling Octopress, 1992), Tail
Spinners, Treeline, and Time For Rhyme. In addition, several were broadcast on CBC
Radio's "Alberta Anthology" on December 15th, 1996.
    My thanks to the editors for their encouragement and support.

Published in 1999 by: **Ekstasis Editions Canada Ltd.**,Box 8474, Main Postal Outlet,
Victoria, B.C. V8W 3S1

The Canada Council for the Arts since 1957	Le Conseil des Arts du Canada depuis 1957

Nothing Definite Yeti has been published with the assistance of a grant from the Canada
Council and the Cultural Services Branch of British

Contents

The Beaked Beast of Bungalow Beach

I'm the Beaked Beast of Bungalow Beach.
To look at my smelly, rotten,
putrifying gelatinous corpse,
it's easy to see how I've gotten
a monstrous reputation, of course,
but once I was lithe;
once I was free.
I frolicked the seas —
a porpoise with purpose —
or something like, without pedigree.
Now you want to tag my bones,
get on the phones,
give me a phylum, a species,
identify my family tree.
Say only this of me:
I got caught in a red tide:
a red cloud of toxic plankton
got in my food. I am sadly abused.
I'm the beaked beast of Bungalow Beach.
Some putrefying man-made slime
made that plankton bloom.
Fish fed on the plankton;
I fed on the fish.
Simply to die with grace
is now my only wish.

The Beazel

In Lake Superior, Near Sault Ste. Marie,
where the water is dark and frigid and deep,
there lives the strangest fish you'll ever see —
a very rare fish — with fur worth a heap!

This torrid lil' trout they call a beazel
has a svelter pelt than ermine or weasel.
You'd swear it was a Persian Catfish and purred,
it's so luxuriantly and sumptuously furred.

No kidding! I saw a stuffed one on a wall
in a small coffee shop in Agawa.
Really! A block from town hall.
Drop by — or call Fisheries in Ottawa.

They say these beazels are really mutants,
are chock full of industrial pollutants —
cadmium, lead, and mercury;
polyvinyl chlorides and PCBs.

They got a muddy, disagreeable taste,
run silent and deep as nuclear subs
powered, I suppose, by factory waste,
and discharge whenever they rub.

But what a blast! What a gas! How neat
when male and female beazels meet.
Their hackles glow and spark and crackle
like some Van der Graff tabernacle!

They ain't shy or coy or even discrete,
but court and spark in the spawning grounds
like anions and cations in heat,
and — Lord! — they make such yowlin' sounds!

Imagine havin' baked beazel for lunch.
Talk about toxic! I have a hunch
our chromosomes would go akilter or tilt,
our eyes 'd divide like eggs in milt;

or maybe we'd just acquire a charge,
give gigowatt kisses that lit up the eyes
of some languorous Larry, Ethel or Marge,
give them an amorous ampere surprise.

The very werewolf of fishes, the beazel —
Twice as sneaky as any ol' weasel.
Catch a hot fur-bearin' trout,
who knows what change may come about?

Benbecula

(*To the tune of* Be-Bop-a-Lula)

Ben-be-cu-la, she's my baby.
Ben-be-cu-la, I don't mean maybe.
Ben-be-cu-la, she's my mermy maid, my mermy maid
my mermy maid.

She's the maid of the He-bri-des.
She's the queen of all the seas.
She's the one the Grimnis folk adore.
She's the one of Sgeir na Duchadh shore.

She's the one that's got the finny beat.
She's the one with tail instead of feet.
She's the one that swims so close to shore.
She's the one that sings the songs of yore.

(*Repeat Chorus*)

Well, the ladies cuttin' seaweed
ain't got the moves I need,
They're jealous and they're dim;
Can't do the swish or swim.

They're dour and malodorous;
ain't rhythmic or melodious.
Wear galoshes and old weeds —
I can't stand their scarves or tweeds.

(*Repeat Chorus*)

The men they tried to catch her,
but none of them could match'er.
She swam right through their net;
ain't no one caught her yet.

Though they stoned her in the water,
hit her conk before she bought 'er,
she's no one's lumpen daughter
and still my spritely otter.

(*Repeat Chorus*)

The Buru

(*Naga-Uta*)

Buru you call us,
after our deep mournful cries.
We're almost extinct,
thanks to your need for more rice.
You filled in our swamps,
forced our retreat to deep pools.
Filled the pools with rocks,
crushing most of our number
into fine bone dust.
How were we a nuisance then?
What could we have done?
We ate a little swamp weed,
gave birth to live young,
bellered to our creator,
lay out in the sun.
We were large, peaceful lizards
with languorous ways.
We didn't steal your children,
never killed for fun.
Could you not have let us be?
Channeled some water
to terraced paddies elsewhere?
True, one of our clan
wrapped his tail around a man,
dragged him to his death
in the placid, deep, still lake,
but only after
he shot one of our children.

Now all is silence.
The few of us who live still
keep to deeper ponds
a valley or two away
from you monstrous beasts
of the Apis Tanis clan.
Like huge crocodiles
with only nostrils showing,
we keep our distance —
huge pickles in a barrel —
lollygag and drift.
And the misty mountain clouds
of the still remote
Himalayas of Assam
part like frail curtains.
Buru! Buru! we bellow,
and bring forth the sun.

Champ,
The Monster of Lake Champlain

Well, thum folks gawk and gape,
and thum folks thtop to oggle;
thum drop their jawth 'n' chin-wag,
talk zeuglodon boondoggle.

Thum think I'm a crypto-dino —
thum prehithtoric critter
with flippers four and neck galore —
thum genetic chromo thplitter.

thum thigh at my glittering thcaleth
that flath thilver in my wake;
otherth thwear I'm olive green —
a mammal, for heaven'th thake!

Thum thay I'm a terrible therpent,
ath thick ath a telephone pole;
I hith to my kith with a lithp,
thurprithe theep 'n' thwallow 'em whole.

Thum thay I croon like a loon,
or bawl like a bellicothe moothe.
They quake at my tonthular tenor
when I thtreth and let loothe.

Yeth, I got thum freaky deviathun
in my theptum and my thellth.
Gonna thplath and undulate thum.
Gonna curl their white lapelth.

The truth ith that I'm thy;
my lithp ith tho darn thilly
I'm embarrathed all the time
and can't thcare a tiger lily.

Though I try on different costumth
'n play the monthrouth pother,
I make only brief appearantheth
for I'm jutht a therpent hother.

The Olitau and Ahool

In western Java
on the slopes of Salak
there lives an animal
most loathsome and black.

Its face is like a dog's
that chases parked cars;
you'd swear it was a monster
from Venus or Mars.

Its feet point backwards,
and, though it prefers fish,
it finds man a delectable,
tasty alternate dish.

Men call it the Ahool,
after its piercing cry.
Pray you don't hear it;
you don't need to know why.

But since you ask, I'll say —
and swear, by God, its true —
the Ahool is a monster bat
the size of a kangaroo.

It has the wingspan of a condor,
the teeth of a baboon.
Few folks have seen one;
pray you do not soon.

The few sad fools who've tried
to catch this beast at its ease
have ended up inside it
or flayed from head to knees.

It's got a nasty cousin too:
the Olitau of Cameroon.
Don't think you'll catch it napping
near some pool or lagoon.

The Olitau only mutters
a gruff perfunctory *unch,*
and that is almost always
after it has lunch.

Hiachuckaluck*

Hiya, Hiachuckaluck.
How's it hangin'? How's yer luck?
Howza about some halibut?
Hope yer not too fonda folks
full of fat and artichokes.

Hiya, Hiachuckaluck.
How's the wife and little chucks?
Can I offer my mukluks,
Try a bucketful of kippers.
People taste real bad with zippers.

Hiya, Hiachuckaluck.
Want some sirloin? Like some chuck?
Boat bottom roughage is so tough.
Hard to swallow too, I hear.
Have half an arsa grade-A steer.

Hiya, Hiachuckaluck.
Howza about some Arctic duck?
Easy chewing, won't get stuck.
Folks are tough as hockey pucks.
Bad for hiachuckalucks.

 * Hiachuckaluck is the West Coast
Salish name for the beloved
Cadborosaurus, a sea serpent
that haunts Pacific coastal waters.

The Dover Demon

Well, they call me the Dover Demon,
say I got wicked, mischievous ways,
But I just eat roots 'n' berries;
don't want no Massachusetts' fillets.

Yeah. Ain't stokin' on no noxious weeds.
Ain't stinkin' up nobody's face.
Sorry your pop can bopped off my pate, babe.
Guess I best shuffle off to some other place.

In Canada they got better manners —
at least the Cree did some time ago.
Mannegishi they called me and smiled.
Said saucer trickster woncha put on a show?

Well, I got down on all fours to please 'em.
Yeah. I slipped in and out of their tribes,
a cosmic telemetrist trickster supreme-o.
I was respected for my mannegish jibes.

Now you look at my egg-shaped head, babe,
run me to ground like some new world ape,
as if I belonged to some primitive race, eh,
wanted you to simper and gibber and gape.

Now who is the sideshow attraction —
we impish telemetrist teachers
or you swag-bellied, snoose-droolin',
stinky indigenous creatures?

D'Sonoqua

Stomp stomp D'Sonoqua,
hairy from foot to conkua,
played the honky tonkua.

Sweatier than a broncoa,
she drank a bottle of plonkua,
then she hadda honkua.

Not even a barnyard donkua
or half-rotten conchua
is as funky as a D'Sonoqua.

Stomp stomp D'Sonoqua,
ripe from foot to conkua,
assailed her nostonqua.

That's some skunk funkua,
mused the portly punkua.
I best wash in the Wonkua.

So she washed in the river Wonkua
and cleaned off the fetid honkua,
then swore off the squamous plonkua.

Now Stomp stomp D'Sonoqua,
hairy from foot to conkua,
plays only stygian fonkua.

El Chupacabras (The Goatsucker)

Well, down in Puerto Rico
where the sun shines high and bright,
they say a ghastly creature's
got the government uptight.

Its grabbin' goats and headlines.
Suckin' blood 'n' slime;
its drainin' stoats and rabbits,
nabbin' poultry 'n' prime time.

Oh, Chew-chew chu-pa-ca-bra,
you quill pig kanga-ra-too.
you're a vampire most macabre,
a real red-eyed nosferatu.

Chew-Chew chu-pa-ca-bra.
You wallaby wannabe,
you got yourself a mohawk,
now you're on a killing spree.

(*Do Wop Chorus:*)

> *Chew chew chew,*
> *Chu Chu-pa-ca-bra.*
> *Gonna nab nab nab*
> *a new ewe 'n' skedaddle.*

> *Gonna suck suck suck*
> *suck its succulence.*
> *Gonna hop hop hop*
> *over any wall or fence.*

We draw your picture for the paper
but when we draw a bead,
you drop a dirty stink bomb,
our eyes they almost bleed!

Your fiery eyes can hypnotize,
your wicked farts just wreak!
You grab a sheep, go on the lam;
we cannot move or speak.

Chew-chew chu-pa-ca-bra,
you ain't known to palaver;
you leave the nasty callin' card
of a vampire or cadaver.

Chew-chew chu-pa-ca-bra
from whose coffin did you crawl?
Did you catch a flying saucer,
Were you ever here at all?

(*Repeat Chorus*)

They say you ain't no giant,
sport fangs like some ol' snake;
but you sho' don't stop to rattle,
and you doan clean up yo' plate.

Are you on a liquid diet, man?
You sho' love dem sanguine shakes
You leave bodies flat as wineskins
Are you sure you won't eat steaks?

A goat is a just goatskin, eh?
cows are just fat coats;
you leave their fur containers
like quickly quaffed vanilla floats.

The blood runs thick and slow,
as ice cream down a glass.
Your wipe your lips, lick fingertips,
drop dem empties in the grass.

(*Repeat Chorus*)

Emela Ntouka

In the Lake Tele swamplands of Zaire
there dwells a creature cruel and rare
as monstrous as any monster born
with tree-trunk legs and horrid horn.

Emela Ntouka, the pygmies say,
is cantankerous and gets her way.
She bellows and roars and stomps about,
for she's the queen — there is no doubt!

And if any hipster hippo on the make
decides to crash this babe's clam bake,
she skewers his gizzard like shish kebab
and leaves his corpulent corpse to bob.

As quick as its punctured ego deflates,
it bloats and floats past pearly gates
to join the angel band of Ella's phunts,
who thought that they could pull such stunts,

for, dig, this is Toothy Ntouka's 'hood,
you best get that fact understood.
Find yer own crib, Jim; go fish or swim,
unless you're some hunky Ntouka him.

There's only one Ntouka cat can blow
his horn in this fetid fen, and you know
this ain't no crusty Cretacean gig.
Emela's man lives! He's hot; he's big!

And when Nasty Ntouka does the swim,
all the phunts 'n' hippos bug out, Jim,
cos he's one mean green centrosaur,
gonna cut a rug to his hep score.

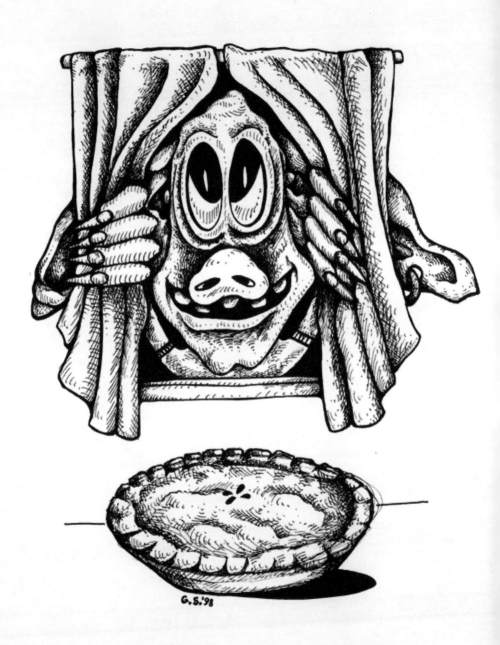

The Mad Gasser of Mattoon

I'm the mad gasser of Mattoon;
I wear a gas mask every full moon.
When you're asleep
I start to creep
like some creature in a cartoon.

When you're zonked out and snore,
I sneak up to your window or door,
pump in a little gas,
which will soon pass,
leave you stiff, headachy, and sore.

Come morning, you'll feel so sick
you'll want some medicine quick,
see your physician,
a real magician,
who knows what does the trick.

He'll send you to the pharmacy,
and there, smiling, I'll be,
ever-ready to fill
his script for the pill
that will rid you of your malady.

The prescription, sorry to say,
may cost you half a day's pay,
but that is the price
of feeling so nice
after I've put in a full day.

The Fouke Monster

An ol' hirsute houdini from Fouke
was reputed to be quite a spook.
a sasquatch-like geek,
he was known by his reek,
which made even the rankest skunks puke.

Well, he'd skulk and tromp through the bogs
and would freak out the hunters' huge dogs.
Just a threatening scowl
or blood-curdling howl,
and the critters'd skitter like frogs.

Now, some folks from the county agreed
such a tourist attraction might need
a few sheep from the fold
to attract the pure gold
of a lucrative film spot or lead,

so they slaughtered some gamy old ram,
then set up a cheap video cam;
had a guy in a suit
run around and look cute
as a sasquatch who scammed on the lam.

When the movie fans came to the show,
they were proud they could part with their dough.
Just to see their own ape
made the gullible gape
and bought backers and hackers Bordeaux.

Gigantopithecus

Could an ancestor of Gigantopithecus
really elude or avoid us this long?
Could it still live peaceably among us,
eat yak meat, berries, roots, Souchong?

Is this the famed Dzu-teh, largest of yeti?
Yowie, Yag-mort, Sasquatch, or Mapinguary?
Seven-foot hairy man-beast, alpha-Betty
that has enthralled, scared, made men wary?

A gruff old lummox that jumps up and down,
but can only hoot, "*Eugh! Eugh! Eugh! Eugh!*"
Mimic birds and babies crying, gawk or frown
when confronted with creatures like me or you?

And why shouldn't it chase us from its cave,
given the way the sons of Adam and Eve behave?

The Gillygaloo

The gillygaloo, my buckeroo,
is shy and reclusive,
all but elusive —
not a bird you can paddle,
or even pole up to
in a punt or canoe.

You'll not catch 'em napping
while out backpacking
in Mexico, Brazil, or Peru,
for many a zoo
hasn't got near
the vigilant gillygaloo.

It's far too reclusive
to pose for exclusives,
will have no truck,
absolutely no traffic
with National Geographic
or any shutterbug crew.

Drop in on a bungy
to some grotty and grungy
rookery out on a ledge,
you're apt to find eagles,
condors or seagulls,
not the bashful gillygaloo.

No. Mr. Gillygaloo makes no hullabaloo
when it comes to building a nest.
He needs no nook or ledge
from which to hang ten
or build a new den
for Ms. Gillygaloo and her brood.

Indeed, any slope'll do —
the steeper, the better,
to continue unfettered,
For a gillygaloo must vamoose
when it hears a man puffing
up the steep grade to its nest.

Its eggs are most portable,
can't roll or slip from its knees.
The reason, you see,
is they are not oval or round,
but cubic and stackable —
even in a gale force breeze.

Seriously. Ask a lumberjack and see.
Hardboiled gillygaloo eggs
were once used as dice
on cold winter nights
when the men gambled away
their packets of pay.

Anyone who had a gillygaloo egg
was said to get giddy and lose.
Who knows? Maybe it was the way
the greenhorns would play —
without a full deck,
or — heck — maybe it was the booze.

Tell you what though:
give this coin a throw.
Heads I win; tails you lose —
the next guy through that door
will back up my story,
maybe even tell you some more.

Globsters

We ain't no two-bit hoods,
ain't tryin' to fence no goods;
ain't no natty dread head mobsters,
don't eat no steaks or lobsters.
Yeah, we gots no dolls or Doras,
don't wear zoot suits or fedoras;
we ain't gonna read your auras.
We're globsters! Ye-ah, globsters!

We're not fishy or amphibious,
but completely cartilaginous.
Gots no toes or noses;
can't strike no fancy poses.
Gots no tender tensile tentacles;
can't open or close no ventricles.
We're completely asymmetrical.
We're globsters! Ye-ah, globsters!

Gonna glom right onto you;
gonna stick to you like glue.
Gonna give your hair a muss:
gonna ooze and flow like pus.
Ain't no yours or mine —
gonna cover you in slime;
gonna love you all the time!
We're globsters! Ye-ah, globsters!

We gonna stink up all yo' beaches,
befuddle all yo' teachas.
No phylum can contain us;
no scientist can name us.
Hold your hats and phones:
we gots no skulls or bones,
Don't make no swaps or loans.
We're gobsters! Ye-ah, globsters!

We gots no fingers or phalanges;
we old as the Amazon or Ganges.
Ain't gonna swim or spawn;
just gonna float along,
rise from the deep sea ocean
whenever we get the notion.
Ain't no ambergris or lotion:
We're globsters! Ye-ah, globsters!

We not big; we huge,
but we gots no attitudes.
We ride the swelling tide,
arrive where the seas decide.
We ain't fussy 'bout what we eat —
flora, fauna, fish, or meat:
our proteins are complete.
We're globsters! Ye-ah, globsters!

De Loys Ape

Now scientific wisdom holds
no native American ape
has ever graced our jungles
to jibber, jabber, or jape.

The only tailless monkeys here,
we are assured by those most wise,
drink beer and hang from rafters,
chafe at shirts and paisley ties.

But deep in the jungles of Venezuela,
near the shores of Lake Maracaibo,
there lives a dreaded monster ape
the village folk all know.

Ameranthropoides loysi —
named for geologist F. De Loys,
whose unwary crew discovered it
while making too much noise.

Now this ape has got some habits
you best take the time to learn:
he don't like folks to stare at him
or his head'll take a turn.

He'll go from nonchalant and cool
to violent fearsome beast,
grab a branch and club your head
until your skull is nicely creased.

and if he is outnumbered,
he'll pelt you with his poop,
scoop fresh-squeezed gooey handfuls
from his anus with a whoop.

You'll find yourself bespattered
head to foot with his hello,
and you know that sloppy goop
won't smell like fruit jello.

Small wonder, given this
most unseemly etiquette,
that his better, homo s,
hasn't bagged this critter yet.

Oh, De Loys' boys they shot one,
and took a photo of the beast,
but no one would believe him
when the picture was released.

The ape looked like a five-foot gibbon
with round orbits and no tail,
sat propped up on a packing crate,
slack-jawed but looking hale.

Put a suit and tie on him,
prop him at some bar,
he might not look as simian
as some drunk with stub cigar.

Llamighan Y Dwr

(*Decastitch*)

The lovely jewelled winged snake,
Llamighan Y Dwr of Glamorgan,
lay coiled in languorous loops one day.
Its thoughts opaque, it lay awake;
its gem-like scales transfixed a man,
who, dazzled, led his flock astray.
So hypnotized was he with glitz,
he scarcely saw the snake unwind
and squeeze the life and take the wits
of all the lambs on which it dined.

Hoop Snakes
(Rhupunt)

If you go out,
be sure to scout
the hills about
for dread hoop snakes.

They bite their tails,
roll hills and dales,
the deep wood trails,
and have no brakes.

Stay in shape,
don't gawk or gape
or you'll not 'scape
its deadly bite.

The only way
to get away —
a bit risqué —
is to hang tight,

dive through the hoop
or scream and whoop
and quickly scoop
the rolling ring

with branch or stick,
then fling it quick
into a crick,
or maybe swing,

ringtoss the freak
to cruel hooked beak
of some sneak sleek
hawk on loft wing.

That ravenous
raptor won't fuss
with that dang cuss,
but squeeze its guts

like toothpaste,
or just lambaste
the beast posthaste —
no ifs, ands, buts,

and then will feast
on what it's greased,
parcelled and pieced
for its lil' jakes.

But if you're bold,
you can take hold
of tail, I'm told,
and twirl the snake

until it's straight,
dizzy, prostrate,
and smash its pate
against a rock.

Excorticate,
exhoopitate —
just one quick knock,
that's all it takes.

Hypertrichosis

Harry Harmon was so hairy
and his hormones so contrary
he had a full beard at fourteen
the like of which no one had seen.

The hair grew so far down his neck
he soon decided — what the heck —
he may as well just braid the thatch
as shave it from his chest hair patch.

One woolly eyebrow bridged his nose;
he had hairy knuckles and hairy toes
and so much hair upon his back
he became more flaxen than a yak.

Now Harry ain't no canine lupus
or teen werewolf or hirsute doofus,
though lithe and lean and muscular;
he wanted to date and drive a car.

So put yourself in Harry's place —
imagine getting up to shave your face,
spending a fortune on cans of Nair
in a desperate bid to remove your hair.

He tried expensive depiling creams,
electrolysis and hairbrained schemes.
Nothing would rid him of his hair;
his social life, it went nowhere.

He began to look so like a forest,
he even thought of agent orange.
Life was a drag, the total pits.
The only good thing was hidden zits.

Yeah, some guys get acne real bad;
it depresses 'em and makes 'em sad.
Some girls got to binge and purge,
look like zombies, sing a dirge.

But he's got something ten times worse,
some wicked badass gypsy curse.
Yeah, say it: hyper tri - cho - sis,
badder than a bad case of halitosis.

T-t-t-t-t too much hair!
Yeah, it's sproutin' everywhere!
Even on his feet and palms;
can't even collect alms.

T-t-t-t-t too much hair!
Folks have to stop and stare.
Gonna get himself a complex;
can't undo Ma Nature's hex.

Ah! But Harry ain't no dummy.
He found a way to make 'em chummy.
Bought himself a Stratocaster,
made himself a guitar master.

Yeah! Hold your hats and phones!
That ain't no metal thrash Ramones
playing three-chord boogie on the stand;
that's the Hairy Hormone band!

Yeah! Pump up the volume, Jack,
and cut this cat some slack;
he's gonna rock 'n' roll and rhyme
like some 'lectric porcupine.

Gonna shake that flaxen hair
til it sticks out everywhere;
gonna sing the blues and moan,
cut more discs than you can own.

Gonna play them riffs and chops
til the moon gets up and bops.
Ain't gonna be 'buked or scorned,
whether hairy, fanged, or horned.

Got the boogie fever, Jim;
now the girls all flock to him
cos he's the harmony cat
and his Hormones is playin' fat,

singin' Hypertrichosis,
ain't no hairy dis;
Hypertrichosis,
ain't no great abyss.

Gonna bathe in that shampoo.
Gonna croon and moan for you.
Gonna get get myself a perm.
Gonna make my belly firm.

Who's got too much hair?
Don't need no underwear.
Who's too hirsute, Jim?
Ain't I neat and trim?

Hypertrichosis,
ain't no hairy dis.
Hypertrichosis,
ain't psoriasis.

T-t-t-t-t too much hair!
Go ahead and stare!
T-t-t-t-t too much hair,
sproutin' everywhere!

The Jersey Devil

In the Pine Barrens of New Jersey
in seventeen thirty-five
there lived a harried housewife
and her harried husband, Clive.

"Mother" Leeds was Mary's name —
a name she earned in spades,
for eleven children waited
when the midwife drew the shades.

"I'm sick of kids!" their Momma cried.
"Let this twelfth one be the devil!"
And, sure enough, a devil was born,
if the midwife was on the level.

She says she saw it, cried "My God!"
and fainted straight away.
The devil then unfolded wings
and flew the coop that day.

But not before Clive and the kids
heard an awful, mournful call,
came running from the fields to see
cloven hoofprints in the hall.

They could hardly believe their eyes:
it defied all common horse sense
to see a 'roo with wings and hooves
drooling lasciviously on the fence.

Other people have seen it since,
or heard its banshee shriek;
lost many a barnyard animal
when it strayed too near the creek.

Now Moms and Dads throughout the land
pack shotguns in their cars,
and for the smaller broods they have,
they thank their lucky stars.

Kongamato!

From the far northeastern border
of the fetid Jiunda swamp
to the eerie eyries of the Lukanga
where intrepid travellers tromp

there lives a Mesozoic monster,
a terrifying Pterosaur
with leathery wings and featherless hide,
blood-red eyes and teeth galore.

Kongamato, to the Zambian crew:
killer of livestock, breaker of boats;
it screeches and screams; rules supreme.
Rends flesh from bone, tears out throats;

lets not so much as an intestine by,
unless a croc snaps 'er up first,
then skims the water gracefully
to gargle 'n' slake its thirst.

Kongamato! Kongamato! the wide-eyed
fisherfolk scream from their pirogues.
Kongamato! Evil beast, spare us please!
But no: women, children, saints, rogues

all taste the same to this unflappable
bat-winged Pterodactyl terrorist.
What it can't eat on the wing
it carts to its cave in scaly fist.

One-fisted human soda pop — crack,
off pops your head like a bottle cap;
a long draught of blood from the neck
and — ah! — it's time for a Konga nap.

The Kraken

The Bishop of Bergen, Erik Pontopiddan
writes of the Kraken, for so long hidden
beneath the roiling perturbable waves
of many unfortunate mariners' graves,

that its back — slimy and vile —
bigger around than a nautical mile —
looks like an island, black and bare,
forlorn and pitiless as a dead man's stare.

But around this isle hanks of weed
bob and weave with a horrible need,
as though a bed of kelp were breathing,
some thought beneath its net were seething.

Each Kraken eye, make no mistake,
is bigger than a dinner plate;
its suckers, in neat rows of two,
can hold more forks than me or you.

It's terror and fear of this Kraken
that makes a bo's'n's sails slacken,
for very few sailors who've seen one
have seen their wits outsail the sun,

for the Kraken can snap and make dice
of any man's bones in a trice,
and toss them aside as the captain bemoans
the loss of his crew to Davey Jones.

Aye, and a midden of bones becomes grist,
sifts through a man's fingers like mist,
but the Kraken still measures size
by the distance and white of men's eyes.

Ballad of the Beast of Le Gevaudan

Daughter, daughter, where are you going?
O do not walk so fast.
Speak, speak to your doting father,
Or else I shall be lost.

The night was dark; I prayed for you there.
Now I am wet with dew.
The slope was steep, and I did weep
When I met the loup garou.

Daughter, daughter, what can I say?
O do not leave so soon.
Stay, daughter, say what tore your heart away
Beneath this gibbous moon.

Father, the air was thick with fog and mist.
A sheep had strayed; I looked for it
O'er hill, in dale... My father, I have failed.
A wolf, I fear... My ribs, it split.

Daughter, daughter, my heart is rent as well.
What man or beast could do this deed?
What wolf attack a lamb, then eat
the heart of a sweet girl? What creed —

Shhh, let your heart be still, my liege.
Let it rest as moonlight in the dew.
I once was yours, and now I am forsaken;
I must bid you and this world adieu.

Alas, not so soon, my sweet, my petite chou.
The world is old and you are young —
Would that I could see thee wed betimes,
And sing, before angels take thy tongue.

Pity instead the beast of Le Gevaudan,
A creature that hath come from hell:
Half man, half wolf; its heart is twain.
It belongs to the moon as well.

Tell me, whither shall you go, my dear,
That we cannot follow thee and see?
Will it be heaven, then, or some fen
The beast hath madly offered thee?

That the creature hath my heart, 'tis true,
And my body, torn asunder, cannot mend.
But where my soul departeth to, and when,
I cannot say, but walk the next bend.

Shall I walk a while with thee then?
O daughter, daughter, say I may.
I've mourned too long in these heavy robes;
My heart is heavy; I cannot stay.

Oh father, would that you could. We two might
linger long in this valley without veil.
But, alas, I cannot tarry and must go alone.
A light beckons; my spirit hath set sail.

The Nandi Bear

Now there's nothing namby pamby
about your nasty Nandi Bear;
he ain't no napping Panda
with natty nappy hair.

He's got no cuddly rumbly tumbly
like your cartoon cutie Pooh,
and he don't dine on eucalyptus
or sit around and chew bamboo.

He's got no cutesy putesy eyepatch
like your Victor terrier;
he ain't listenin' for his master,
sittin' pert on derriere.

Oh, he'll sit back on his haunches
like your black bear in a zoo.
He'll shamble and he'll ramble,
but he won't beg or mug for you.

No. The Nandi is demanding —
most wicked and insistent.
When it's time to gnash or nosh,
He's terribly consistent:

It's strictly brains for this bear —
trepanned, warm, and fresh;
offal is a gnawful and simply awful;
he don't chaw on bones or flesh.

A gormand, yes; a surgeon, no.
One clean swipe removes a face,
and a brain is quickly hulled
without muss or fuss or trace.

A.K.A. the Chemosit of Kenya,
the Nandi ain't no Gentle Ben or dandy,
so when it comes to eatin' irons,
he uses claws because they're handy.

Eating with the hands in Africa
is not considered rude,
and while monkey brains are a delicacy
and homo sapiens brains tabooed,

no one's gonna accuse a Nandi
of breaching etiquette
or forgetting to wipe his face
with a napkin or serviette.

While his manners require upgrading,
and Emily Post might thump her text,
the Nandi think they're dandy,
and one man as good as the next.

Megamouth

(*to be read in an Edward G. Robinson
gangster style voice*)

Well, old Edward G.
got nothin' on me.
When he bid his moll
come hither with "doll,"
or lizard-like crook
of a finger or look,
she came runnin',
no matter how stunnin' —
Oh yeah, baby,
he don't mean maybe;
his wide, grouper kisser
never ever missed 'er.
And I get no stain
from any who would deign
put a barbed hook in me
while trollin' in the sea,
cos I'm the top dog;
I set eyes agog
when you land me on deck
with all yer high tech
fish-findin' gear, see.
We ain't talkin' debris.
Get near my great maw
I'll surely take a chaw
outta yer sorry mug,
like you was Red Man plug.
You'd fit like a stogey
in the lips of this fogy,
so back off, Jack,

and cut me some slack.
I may be
a bottom feeder, see,
but you're just a pup;
I'd suck you right up
like a vacuum cleaner,
eat you like a wiener,
if I took a notion,
cos this is my ocean.
I'm the boss here.
Do I make myself clear?

Megascoliedes

Now yer megascoliedes are huge
and they love to tunnel and scrouge.
You gotta be astute; can't stand around
and look cute in these hot latitudes,
if you wanna view its cool thews.

Seven feet is a lotta length to accrue
a wiggly earthworm attitude through.
No time to snooze if you don't wanna lose
your grip or loop 'round its gooey girth
cos they ooze like toothpaste from a tube.

Seven feet of pure peristaltic power
gonna pull you into some mulish
tug-a-war too, you bet. So you best
listen up and move when I say move.
This worm's got its own groove to pursue.

To get the drop on this wicked worm
you can't make a lot of noise or squirm;
you gotta learn where in the earth
to apply that electric current to
to jolt 'em silly and make 'em firm.

You gotta give 'em the juice,
so they get down and get loose,
do the funky scrooge and get-up-with-it groove,
shake and shimmy like bony maroney,
and come out of their holes like periscope hose.

When they do the herky jerky and get loose,
slap a cable round 'em in a noose;
when they're flaccid, they get placid.
Pull tight and haul with all your might.
You've got to drag 'em out in plain sight.

Seven feet a worm is gonna squirm,
so clamp'em and zap 'em fast,
then stand back while they go through
an alphabet of noodle shapes.
They boogie 'til they're truly cooked.

Seven feet of smokin' worm'll hurt
and pass a good two yards a dirt,
so stand back 'til they're good and limp —
all seven feet of protein gimp.
megascoliedes ain't so neat 'n' tidy.

Once they're dead, whaddaya do?
Well, we cross-section 'em for barbecue
or wind 'em on a spool and freeze'em;
use the truck winch 'n' hook to catch
great whites and makos when they're bitin'.

They like to tug and tussle and squirm,
so we lay out the cable 'n' hook the worm
way out on the sandbar at low tide,
then sit and wait for the water to rise,
winch 'em in slowly, play 'em a bit.

Sometimes it takes two trucks in tandem —
even three to play and land 'em;
a good size great white don't mind
a bite a checkerplate, if it decides
to dine on megascoliedes 'n' seat stuffin'.

So you best have yer wits about you,
and a coupla good vehicles and chains.
Watch the roads too. If it rains,
yer traction's not gonna give you
the advantage. Believe me, I know.

Yep. Lost a Nissan to a great white once.
Et the whole dang thing, spat out the plates.
It don't pay you nothin' to hesitate.
But first we need a megascoliedes,
and that could take a month of Fridays.

Mo Mo Motivator

Well, I'm the Missouri Monster, babe.
Yeah, I'm the Missouri Monster, babe.
You know misery is my middle name.

I don't smell much like patchouli.
Yeah, I'm smelly and unruly,
but you know I love you truly.

(*Female back-up singers:*)

Yeah, he's Mo Mo
and he's mo' mo'
motivated
to get hitched and propagated.

Ain't no way you can refuse him.
No. No. Cannot 'buke or 'buse him,
for he's dapper and undaunted:
you know your heart is haunted.

Yeah, I may look like a nasty Rasta,
and all this matted fur just hasta
make you want to pop your pasta,

but if you could can your screamin',
just chill and grasp my meanin',
you'd see my soul's redeemin'.

Yeah, I'd not seem so awful scary;
you wouldn't need to be so wary
just cos I'm no sprite or fairy.

(Repeat female chorus)

Yeah, I could maybe spruce up,
just hork a little juice up,
paste down my bangs and mousse up;

get my fur all permed and curly,
splash on some nice Ben Hurly,
brush my teeth until they're pearly.

Yeah, I'd be your hirsute brute, babe,
and you'd look so pert and cute, babe;
we'd have ourselves a hoot, babe.

(Repeat female chorus)

We'd stomp through swamp and tulies,
cavort 'cross plains and coulees;
I'd mop up my snot and droolies.

You could teach me table manners,
how to wave flags and hang banners;
I'd be the best of family planners.

(Repeat female chorus)

Yeah, we could all the pleasures prove
and rocks and fields and mountains move;
they'd hang our portraits in the Louvres.

I'd be your beast; you'd be my beaut,
and all our critters'd be so cute —
Who cares what science doth refute?

We'd dance the light fandango;
we'd do the Piltdown Tango,
be man and juicy mango.

(*Repeat female chorus and fade*)

Mono Grande

In caves above the jungle floor
of Motto Grosso's deepest green
there lives a creature seldom seen
that's meaner than the Kreen Akore.

Even the Kreen, who stand six four,
and shy away from being seen
by white explorer types, have been
afraid to knock at Mono's door.

They say the monster Mono tears
the tongue out of a victim's head,
has disembowelled many men.

So if you hear one, say your prayers.
You're better scared, than wise and dead;
a legend's best left in its den.

Morag, The Beast of Loch Morar

You know I ain't no skaggy sturgeon,
and those humps you see emergin'
ain't no moilin' mess o' catfish
boilin' water black and churlish;

and while I ain't so young and girlish,
I can still make folks here nervous,
cos I'm Morag, the beast of Loch Morar —
not Nessie, Champ, Chessie, or Betty Noire.

Yeah, you better not toss that hi-test line,
unless you're invitin' my kin here to dine.
Those eel-like critters you caught 'n' tossed
have big white teeth they've brushed and flossed.

They're bigger now 'n' have appetites
for whatever screams, thrashes, or fights,
and love to pick their teeth with planks
from fishermen's boats or splintered shanks.

And as for Nessie's more famous poses —
you can toss her a bouquet of roses,
get tickled pink and flushed and florid,
there ain't no loch monster quite as horrid

as Morag, the black beast of Loch Morar,
whether you come for photos from near or far,
cos I ain't no glitz-giddy movie queen,
but you'll know fear once you've come and seen.

Yeah baby, my moilin' forty feet of coils
gonna put the squeeze on those other goils.
Go on! Lay odds and place your bets —
whatever Morag wants, sweet Morag gets!

That's right. Don't you get cute or funny;
I ain't talkin' a eatin' toast 'n' honey.
I'll take my Scotsmen any way you dress 'em.
Swallow 'em whole and say God bless 'em!

Morgawr

The Brits, they call me Morgawr,
say I'm a sight to see;
I got tough rubbery skin:
no harpoon can hurt me.

Yeah, I got a twenty-foot flexible neck,
I got a head as sleek as a seal's,
I got four fantastic flippers
for skedaddlin' after my meals;

I got three dandy dorsal humps,
a long strong back and tail;
I'm the envy of any sauropod,
sea serpent or ol' whale.

I got Hoover bags for lungs
to holler to me missus,
"Oi, Morgy girl, come hither:
yonder swim sweet dinner fishes!"

> *Chorus:*
>
> *Yeah, ain't no plesiosaur to please you;*
> *don't want no ties that bind.*
> *So you just keep on lookin';*
> *I'll play hard to find.*
>
> *Cos I'm Morgan the Morgawr;*
> *you're more than mortified*
> *to claim you saw a dino*
> *lollygaggin' with the tide.*

All along the Cornwall coast
I travel north and south;
I love to linger languidly,
from Lizard to Falmouth.

So should you spot me cruisin',
just dig my horsey grin;
gimme high five on the flipper;
I'll slip you my cool fin.

Hey, you know I ain't a muggin'
on accounta my good looks;
I'm better off escapin'
your knowledge net and hooks.

(*Repeat chorus*)

Lusca Calypso

Dem say down Andros Island way
off de west Bahamian bay
It have some devil dere
dat sure to raise yer hair.

> *Chorus:*
>
> > *Dis Lusca big and strong.*
> > *Its arms be twelve foot long.*
> > *It fix you wid evil eye;*
> > *your heart go petrify.*

Many an island man
go catch am fish fo' pan.
Dem reach fo' grab de net
and become de Lusca fete.

> (*Repeat chorus*)

'Fore you can scream or shout,
its eight arms be all about
and monkeyfy o'er de mast
like some wicked fish gymnast.

> (*Repeat chorus*)

I remind de time one stop
a two-master wid de prop.
E wrap around de rudder
'n' rock de boat 'n' flood 'er.

(Repeat chorus)

Once de hahnds get hold of you,
you dead, mi mahn, for true.
De Lusca drag you down
and you surely gonna drown.

(Repeat chorus)

Now all de beaches here about
have de white sands buckra tout,
but dey doan know de trut',
dat is bones it constitute.

(repeat chorus and fade)

Nothing Definite Yet!

Mr. Tombazi has seen one,
a tall and hairy and free one —
"Just like a man," he claims,
"Only hairier than uncle James.

"He was walking across the snow,
getting where he had to go.
Not hunched up or bunched up
or dragging his lunch up,

not ambling or shambling,
shilly-shallying or rambling,
but striding, upright and bold,
clapping his sides from the cold.

He strode up that steep slope,
chin up, proud as the pope.
Picked a rhodo. Who can tell?
Maybe stuck it in his hairy lapel.

Nothing was abominable about him,
this hairy man of high Sikkim;
though in the all-together,
he seemed used to the cold weather,

wasn't rude or abusive or mean,
like some tradesmen I have seen.
So, unless nudity's a sin,
I'd say it's time we begin

calling our snowman some name
that doesn't betoken fair game
to hunters and big trophy seekers,
jokers in fat, furry sneakers.

A yeti needs no photo op
to live in peaceful co-op
with his yeti bretheren,
so find another specimen.

The yeti may have evolved from the ape,
but it's not polite to gibber and jape
or gawk at anyone, however dressed,
and the yeti's never been impressed —

not in days of yore or since —
with other simians sizing his prints.
So he's got big feet — big deal!
The better to get to a meal.

So if you're lurking with some Sherpa,
or have struck a deal with some Gurkha
over a bowl of cold spaghetti
to go bag yourself a yeti,

forget it. No one's caught one yet,
no matter what the weave of net
or method of deception he chose.
The snowman knows the way wind blows.

And if you catch a hungry snowman
stealing food or playing showman,
crawl inside your nylon tent;
say it was foul and flatulent.

Say you cannot say for sure,
but it wasn't shy or demure.
Blame a goat, blame a bear;
don't chase it in your underwear!

Say all you could tell for sure
was that it hadn't washed its fur.
Tell 'em the beast was awful sweaty;
smile and say nothin's definite yeti."

Rondeau For a Sleepy Sasquatch

In Boston Bar a Sasquatch stood
And scratched his bottom with some wood.
For all the logged-off trees he'd seen,
The distances were lush and green;

And crossed with shadows and cool brooks,
The moss grew soft, as soft it would.
And so he napped as monsters should,
And slept a monstrous sleep unseen
in Boston Bar.

Then came a-tromping through the bush
A nosy dog and tenderfoot.
Roused the Sasquatch from his sleep,
Snapped the thread of his warm dream.
And nevermore was Sasquatch seen
in Boston Bar.

The Skrelling

Beware the ugly skrelling.
He never cleans his dwelling;
he's smelly and he's hairy;
he's mean and so contrary,
he'd as likely skin and eat you
as nod hello or greet you.

He's always mad or glummy,
don't like to play gin rummy.
You're never gonna please him,
and nothing can appease him,
so you best be armed and wary;
he's a nasty adversary.

He might be four feet tall,
and you know he knows he's small,
but there's no point in getting chummy,
for his teeth are awful scummy
and his saliva's poxy drool
contains a deadly molecule.

He's toxic and he stinks,
has never heard of sinks.
You won't ever catch him bathin',
let alone see him behavin'
like a decent next door neighbour.
Making friends ain't worth the labour.

The elder of an ancient tribe,
he's been known to imbibe.
Best give the man his berth,
if you value time on earth.
He still uses bows and arrows
and patrols the icy narrows.

So when you're out kayaking
or planning on backpacking
in the muskeg near his shack,
be sure to watch your back.
Never forget his evil kith.
Why sally forth if you can sally fifth?

Skunk Ape *

Well, I may be big and chunky,
smell a little ripe or punky,
but I ain't no junkfood junky,
and you know I ain't no monkey.

No, he ain't gonna climb no trees.
Cain't hang from tail or knees.
he ain't no new world ape.
Cain't jibber jab or jape —

Cos I'm the skunk ape!
Ye-ah, that's right, baby.
I'm a hirsute hunka spunk;
I'm the skunk ape!

He don't listen to no Monk;
gotta have that sweet swamp funk
if his heart is gonna pump,
and you know he's gotta jump —

Cos I'm the skunk ape!
Ye-ah, that's right, baby —
big as that tree trunk:
I'm the skunk ape!

Cos I'm the skunk ape!
Don't need no dainty hanky;
gonna hang with Rank and Skanky.
Ye-ah — skunk ape!

Cos he's the skunk ape.
gonna grab your hairy nape;
gonna do the shimmy shake;
gonna stomp and crack and break

those tree brakes in the way,
cos I'm the skunk ape!
Gonna get down, Piltdown,
do the funky skunk ape!

Cos he's the skunk ape!
Don't just gawk and gape!
Do the Bigfoot Boogie;
shiver, shake, and shoogie!

Do the funky Skunk Ape!
Ain't no flatfoot flunky!
Ain't gonna do no monkey!
Do the hunky Skunk Ape!

(*Fade*)

He's a hirsute hunka spunk!
Gotta be that sweet swamp funk
Gotta hunker down and bunk
with his sweet punky mama dunk

and do the skunk ape!
ye-ah, skunk ape...
skunk ape...
skunk ape!

* The skunk ape is Florida's Bigfoot, so named on account of his punky
odor.
Italicized stanzas are for female back-up singers.

Slimy Slim

In Lake Payette in Idaho
there lives a monster you should know.
He ain't no floatin' deadhead, Jim;
the folks they call him Slimy Slim.

Now Slimy's got a gator's grin
and fifty feet of slipp'ry skin.
he's black as any inner tube
and loves to give himself a lube.

He rolls, cavorts, plays loop the loop;
is slick as snot or owl poop.
Your chance of netting him at play?
As good as finding thieves that pay!

He'll snatch your fish right off your lines
and sneer at you before he dines,
or rise up like a cobra snake
and slosh your gunwales with his wake.

He's not the sort, I have a hunch,
to ask you out for tea or brunch,
and seldom desires to dine out,
with lots of fish and ducks about.

But if he does, you'll find him coy
and wont to ring the dinner buoy.
you best decline his offer then,
refuse to swim out to his den.

For Slimy Slim's no gentle min;
he's apt to slip you one cold fin,
and when he wants to gormandize,
your boat just gives him exercise.

The Squonk

A rare, reclusive beast, yer squonk —
a glum lil' sponge from tail to conk.
Exudes a mace-like kind of musk
and weeps and wails from dawn 'til dusk.

The reason it weeps so copiously
is that its skin don't fit, you see:
it sags and bags from head to rump
and drags and bunches in a frumpish lump.

So pretty soon its pores get clogged
with all the grit through which it's slogged.
It's got to stop and wet its skin
to clean the sodden bag it's in.

Ol' Ed he thought he caught one once.
He's slow, you know — bit of a dunce.
Snuck up on that po' baleful thing,
bagged the beast 'n' drew the string.

Was tottin' the mournful critter home,
the sun jus' dippin' into gloam,
the squonk a squallin', fit to b' tied,
ol' Ed all soggy from what's inside —

or so he thought 'til he felt
the water drippin' on his pelt.
The bag it felt so empty too,
like mebbe the critter'd bit clean through.

That can't be possible, he figgered,
or I'd a felt'er squirm b'jiggered,
and though the wailin's completely stopped,
I'd a felt 'er if she dropped.

Now while the bag was truly wet,
some o' that mus' be sweat,
ol Ed he figured, scratchin' his head —
like thoughts were burglars come 'n' fled.

But when he opened up that bag,
sure as shootin', that scalliwag
was not inside and 'tweren't no hole
in t'other end from which it stole.

No. I told you, Ed is slow.
There weren't no way the squonk could go
but through the weave, drop by drop,
unless it loosed the string on top.

For that's the way it is with squonks:
they can't be caught with bags or bonks.
You get the drop on one a-fuddle,
it's gonna melt into a puddle.

Yer squonk don't like its baggy skin
and cries for the fit it knows it's in.
An extra bag just makes things worse.
It melts in sorrow: that's its curse.

Small wonder then few can locate
another squonk with which to mate.
They're self-absorbed, morose and vain,
would rather be a spot or stain;

and rare the hunter too is he
who hears a squonk and gets to see
the ugly sluggish squalling lump
of infant protoplasmic bump.

Sucuruju

S ome say the anaconda of the Amazon,
U ncoiled, is seldom forty feet long.
C ould they be wrong? Could a giant anaconda,
U ndulating through the swamp in some somnolent samba,
R each a hundred, or even two hundred feet
I n some hard-to-reach, muggy backwater retreat?
J ust imagine! Phosphorescent eyes the size of dinner plates
U nforgiving, ancient, and wise, hypnotizing its dates...

G igantic isn't the word! Imagine its snores!
I ncredible! They would cause the river to lap its shores!
G as birds and monkeys out of the trees,
A nd bring any mammal nearby to its knees.
N o need to squeeze 'em; it could out-wheeze 'em.
T ake down any beast at fifty paces, gobble 'em easily.
E xit, gallumph along lumpily 'n' greasily.

Ta-Zum-A Boogie

Well, you've heard of sweet Nessie,
the monster of Loch Ness,
and you know ol' Ogopogo
keeps muggin' for the press;

and you hear tell of ol' Champ,
who hails from Lake Champlain,
maybe heard of Manipogo,
who claims three lakes' domain;

but I bet a soggy sawbuck
you've never heard of me,
Ta-Zum-A of Lake Shuswap,
for I'm the crypto queen.

Yeah, if it's hoops and undulation,
great neckline that you want,
you gotta come to Shuswap
to see the humps I flaunt,

for I ain't no sorry saurian,
no fibrillating fish;
ain't no way to hook me,
can't slap me on your dish.

(*female chorus, softly:*)

Sh-sh-sh shake and shimmy,
Sh-Sh-Sh- Shuswap;
Boo-boo-boo-boogie,
boogie 'til you drop.

Yeah, I'm Ta-Zum-A
Got room to zoom around.
Gonna zip and boogie;
ain't sayin' where I'm bound.

But you bet your last boat bottom
I'll frighten and confound,
make you shake and shimmy,
head for shore and kiss the ground.

You'll do the Ta-Zum-A Boogie.
Yeah. Shiver, shake, and clamber.
You'll drop your oars and jawbones,
loosen up and start to stammer.

You'll spu-spu-spu-spu sputter,
sh-sh-shake and shudder;
cry for your sweet mudder,
wish you had anudder

pair of pa- pa- pants to cover
your quiverin' knockin' knees.
Say Ta-Zum-A monster,
oh plea-plea-plea-plea- please,

Don't you mess wid me,
but do the Shu-Shu-Shuswap Bop,
do the Ta-Zum-A Boogie
til my heart goes flippity flop.

(*Repeat chorus, softly*)

Yeah. Forget your horse-head wimps —
those lolligaggin' posers —
they don't deserve the press,
the silly serpent hosers.

If you want to quake and shiver,
if you need to be inspired,
you gotta find a creature
who ain't gonna be retired.

You need to drive to Shuswap
to do the Shuswap Bop;
you need to see Ta-Zum-A
to give your heart the drop.

You'll do the Ta-Zum-A Boogie.
Yeah. Shiver, shake, and clamber.
You'll drop your oars and jawbones,
loosen up and start to stammer.

You'll spu-spu-spu-spu-sputter,
sh-sh-shake and shudder;
cry for your sweet mudder,
wish you had anudder

pair of pa- pa- pants to cover
your quiverin' knockin' knees.
Say Ta-Zum-A monster,
oh plea-plea-plea-plea- please,

Don't you mess wid me,
but do the Shu-Shu-Shuswap Bop.
Do the Ta-Zum-A Boogie.
Show the folks your chicken walk.

(*Repeat Chorus, softly, and fade ...*)

Mngwa

Deep in the jungles of Zaire,
where the white man's seldom been,
lives the most ferocious beast
anyone's ever seen.

Mngwa, "the strange one,"
most-feared, monstrous, hated,
always leaves its victims
completely mutilated:

Heads torn off, eyes white with fear,
arms strewn here, legs dragged there,
and, always, clutched inside a fist,
a twist, a musky, tell-tale hunk of hair.

Some say mngwa's a monster bear,
some claim it's an evil cat;
no one knows for sure,
and that, my friend, is that.

Best you do not know —
or labour to discover
what this Mngwa is —
you just might not recover.

It just might turn out to be —
God forgive the sons of Cain —
Adam run-amok-in-Eden,
Homo sapiens insane.

Hairy Bipedal Hominid Stomp

Well, we're hairy bipedal hominids
with immature egos and active ids
and funky malodorous teenage kids;
we're hairy bipedal hominids.

Stomp   Stomp
          Stomp   Stomp
Stomp   Stomp
          Stomp   Stomp

We tromp through the bog and into the woods,
holler at loggers, abscond with their goods,
and fumigate yuppity neighbourhoods.
Ain't got no Bachelors, Masters, or PhuDs.

Stomp   Stomp
          Stomp   Stomp
Stomp   Stomp
          Stomp   Stomp

We ain't very dainty or debonair
when pickin' nits out of each others hair.
Don't need to dress up: ain't goin' nowhere.
We eat with our hands; don't need silverware.

Stomp   Stomp
          Stomp   Stomp
Stomp   Stomp
          Stomp   Stomp

We got conical noggins water runs off,
Got no supermarkets, but plenty of scoff,
cool mountain freshets from which we can quaff:
don't need to line up like pigs at a trough.

Stomp   Stomp
       Stomp   Stomp
Stomp   Stomp
       Stomp   Stomp

We nosh on salal, fresh berries, and roots.
We'll have none of yer sugar substitutes.
We don't need no glad rags or slickers or boots.
We're happy, hairy, healthy galoots.

Stomp   Stomp
       Stomp   Stomp
Stomp   Stomp
       Stomp   Stomp

Stay out of our faces; go find yer own swamp,
or we'll beller and roar, do the bipedal stomp.
We'll trounce you 'n' bounce you, 'n' give you a womp;
Bash you 'n' smash you 'n' chew you 'n' chomp.

Stomp   Stomp
       Stomp   Stomp
Stomp   Stomp
       Stomp   Stomp

'Cause we're hairy bipedal hominids
with immature egos and active ids
and funky malodorous teenage kids.
We're semi-sentient hominids.

Stomp   Stomp
              Stomp   Stomp
Stomp   Stomp
              Stomp   Stomp

We don't even fit the intelligence grids,
but you betcha that we ain't no invalids;
our kind's been around since the pyramids.
We're hairy bipedal hominids.

(*fade*)

We're hairy bipedal hominids.
Yeah, hairy bipedal hominids.
Hairy bipedal hominids.

Rug Rats

Rug rats in my parlour!
Rug rats in my hall!
Rug rats on the ceiling!
Rug rats wall-to-wall!

Rug rats running hoses!
Rug rats running free!
Rug rats' running noses!
Rug rats running me!

Rug rats in my pockets!
Rug rats in my fridge!
Rug rats breaking sprockets!
Rug rats on the bridge!

Rug rats giving finger!
Rug rats cutting class!
Rug rats who malinger!
Rug rats who can sass!

Rug rats breaking windows!
Rug rats breaking laws!
Rug rats window-grinned O's!
Rug rats dirty paws!

Rug rats making messes!
Rug rats' push-and-shove!
Rug rats wearing dresses!
Rug rats making love!

Rug rats love 'n' hating!
Rug rats with the blues!
Rug rats graduating!
Rug rats in our shoes!

Rug rats in their parlours!
Rug rats in their halls!
Rug rats on their ceilings!
Rug rats one and all.

Homo Sapiens Strut

While the duende of Belize
are pickin' nits and squashin' fleas,
a didi in Guyana
is enjoyin' a banana.

While the shiru in Ecuador
ignores some beastly chore,
the Amazonas' mapinguary
gets mean and more contrary.

While the Maxicoxis' arrows
get close to the rancheros,
the Umahuaca ucumar
are bein' pushed back way too far,

and the retirin' hairy ucu
is really goin' cuckoo
cos the world is a mess
on account of homo s.

Chorus:

Ho Ho Ho oh homo s,
runnin' out of decency,
got no noblesse.

Ho Ho Ho oh homo s,
gotta make a profit,
put the planet in distress.

He's gotta knock the trees down
so he can build a town;
gonna chop it into timber,
gonna make his muscles limber.

Gonna sell timber by the foot now.
Yeah. Build another hoosegow.
Pow pow pow, put the rebels in the ground;
bring in the cows — ow! — sell 'em by the pound.

He'll give the peasants chainsaws,
fill their festered maws;
build taverns in the jungle,
let 'em drink until they stumble.

They'll take home a few piastas,
buy his milk and eat his pastas;
they'll get thin thin thin,
til the labour does 'em in.

(*Chorus again:*)

Ho Ho Ho oh homo s,
runnin' out of patience,
got no largesse.

Ho Ho Ho oh homo s,
stupid furless hominid,
worse than all the rest.

He burns down all the trees,
kills the plants that kill disease;
creates rangeland by brute force,
landscapes a new golf course.

He pollutes the streams and rivers,
destroys the workers' livers;
brings in herds of burger cattle,
gets embroiled in every battle.

He robs every rubber tapper;
when an engine dies, he scraps 'er.
Clear cuts and 'dozes homes,
sells 'em cars and garden gnomes.

He kills off unknown critters,
excommunicates the quitters;
promotes free enterprise,
sells junk food and tells lies.

Ho Ho Ho oh homo s,
destroys the eco-system,
buys an RV and moves west.

Ho Ho Ho oh homo s,
worst monster on the planet,
gonna put it to the test.

(softly now.)

Worst monster on the planet,
from Nome to Budapest;
worst monster on the planet,
man, he sho' is vexed!

Ho Ho Ho oh homo s.
Ho Ho Ho oh homo s.
Ho Ho Ho oh homo s.

The Lawyer

Of all the monsters in the world
that dare bare fang or claw,
none is nearly quite so horrible,
none remotely so deplorable
as a lawyer invoking the law.

A greasy, usurious creature is he,
his handshake colder than filleted fish.
A veritable sultan of sleaze,
he'll stoop low as an inchworm's knees,
eat anything you slap on his dish.

Getting married is a breeze: five dollars please.
Getting divorced will cost more, of course.
And he'll dawdle, wheedle, cajole
before others muzzle up to his bowl,
bleed you of every financial resource.

He'll do anything legal, for a plump fee.
Do it gleefully, brilliantly — and with panache.
Take from the poor? Set a killer free?
Just ask. He'll find the technicality,
as long as you pay stacks of cold cash.

His favourite colour is fresh folding green,
but like a cat in catnip, he loves to roll
in bales of the soiled, autumn-coloured stuff,
and, whatever the colour, never gets enough,
for to make a buck is his primary goal.

More dangerous than any reticulate python,
with twice as many coils to squeeze you;
the seasoned lawyer has more pins
than his pin-striped suit, and more fins
than any slippery barracuda to please you.

His probing proboscis is finer than a mosquito's,
hits the main artery first time, every time,
flags red with the love of fresh blood.
Need to siphon some off? He'll start a flood,
and show you in print it's no crime.

Want to level some virgin timber somewhere?
Put up some condoes, build a golf course?
Need to evict a few grannies or raise the rent?
However noble the cause, whatever your intent,
the monster of monsters will show no remorse.

If there are chins to tickle, wattles to waggle,
varicosed-veined old prattlers to rattle...
If you have a distasteful task
or need a legal eagle's mask,
call the monster of monsters; he'll not tattle —

Nor tarry! For this creature's most wary.
Hold a billfold under his wattled chin,
and it will cast a shadow like a buttercup,
make his head tilt sideways and up,
for — ah! — being Cain's lawyer was no sin.

And of all the monsters in the world since,
none has a more dainty, delicate paw
than a paunchy lawyer just appointed,
for only he, with oils of justice, is annointed,
and that's holy writ. That, my friend, is the law.

Prayer For Fearsome Critters

"God forgive us and we'll forgive you.
We'll forgive each other 'til we both turn blue
and we'll whistle and go fishin' in the heavens."

— John Prine

Glory be to God who giggles on high
for the Goofgang fish who swim reversewise —
may they never get water in their eyes;
and for the Goofus birds who backwards fly —
may they always get where they once flew
and never ever learn where they're going to.
God bless the Billdad, Squonk, Cross-Feathered See,
the Snoligostus, Cutter Cuss, and Hoop Snake —
all the fearsome critters that live half-baked
in the minds of fakirs who laugh with glee —
may they grow telescopic adjustable gams
and crop steep slope grass like God's own lambs.
God bless us and, we promise, we'll bless you.
Bless this planet, Lord, so we can laugh too.

The Author's Notes On Monsters

Late in the process of editing *Why Were All the Werewolves Men?* for press and working out the voices for some of my monsters, I hit upon the idea of using fifties and sixties rock 'n' roll — Elvis's "Heartbreak Hotel," Manfred Mann's "Do Wah Diddy," various Doo Wop and Girl group teen angst tunes — and basic walking blues structures as templates and sources for some of the environmental and urban legend poems in the book. Well, why not? Early rock 'n' roll ("the devil's music," according to our distraught parents) was the favoured medium to deal with protest, and I had a green theme and middle grade — and middle age! — audience in mind.

Eventually, a good number of decent re-writes got cut from the book for various reasons and I found myself with a corpus of poems that might make a reasonable sequel. Inspired by the breakthrough of the rock and blues parodies, I kept writing more of these and trying different song forms and personae or voices. The sequel, *Nothing Definite Yeti*, relies on similar cryptozoological sightings reports, Fortean lore, folklore, urban and various indigenous tribal monster legends sources. Some of my sources and the creatures I discovered are quite obscure. Perhaps a few notes will acquaint the reader with these monsters.

Sea Monsters

Since it is generally believed life began in the sea, I originally started my book with sea creatures. At the head table, *The Morgawr*, according to the people of the Cornish coast in the U.K., is a large, black plesiosaur-like monster with a two-humped back. Though much disputed, a reasonably clear photo of it exists.

The *Kraken* and its cousin *Lusca* (or Lucsa in some sources) are believed to be giant octopi or squid which haunt the Atlantic and

Carribean regions respectively. They were both feared by sailors and were said to snatch men off the sailing ships of yore and even climb the rigging, thus flooding and capsizing many a boat and drowning many a ship's mate. Few lived to tell the tale.

Globster is the name given by scientists to the various unidentified cartilaginous or monstrous invertebrate creatures whose gristly or gelatinous and foul remains keep turning up on the planet's beaches. Some of these are almost certainly basking shark or giant octopus or squid remains, but many suggest unknown giant mollusks. *The Beaked Beast of Bungalow Beach* appears to be an unknown mammal the size of a whale and turned up on the west coast of Africa in the early part of this century.

Megamouth is a huge wide-mouthed bottom-feeding shark, only recently discovered. Seen dead on, its face really will remind you of an Edward G. Robinson caricature. Edward G., incidentally, for those of you too young to know, was a Hollywood actor famous for his gangster/ bad guy portraits in such classic films as *Key Largo* and *Little Caesar*.

Hiachuckaluck is a monster you may have met before in *Why Were All the Werewolves Men?* There, you met him by his twentieth century moniker, *Cadborosaurus*. The native peoples of the west coast met him much sooner than the white man did and knew him by this other name. Of course, there are about eight or nine descriptions and cryptozoologists suspect there are as many distinct unknown sea serpent or sea monsters out there: a long neck, a merhorse, a many-humped monster, a super eel, a super otter, a marine saurian, a many-finned creature, and a yellow bellied monster; and the first four have been spotted in Canadian waters!

Benbecula is in a class by herself. She is reputedly a real mermaid, and what happened to her supposedly really happened. I've hammed up the details rock 'n' roll style in the first half of the poem and the details are exactly as I found 'em.

Fresh Water Monsters

There are many more than eight of these! I've selected a few famous and not-so-famous ones. *Champ of Lake Champlain* is arguably the most famous. Earlier centuries have her pegged as a giant aquatic eel or snake, but recent sighting reports describe her in plesiosaur and zeuglodon terms. A plesiosaur, of course, is a four-flippered, long-necked dinosaur, and a zeuglodon is a primitive prehistoric whale. Whale? Plesiosaur? Lake serpent? Either Champ is a master of disguises or there is more than one unknown critter in them thar waters!

Morag, of Scotland, and *Ta-Zum-A* of Lake Shuswap, a valley east from the Okanagan's *Ogopogo*, are two lesser-known lake monsters known to the local citizenry, but they appear to be more camera shy than either the *Ogopogo* or *Nessie*, though those who have seen them describe similar creatures.

Slimy Slim hails from Lake Payette in Idaho, and is a smaller — though large! — version of a lake serpent.

The *Beazel* or *Fur-Bearing Trout* is a critter of tall tales. Many is the bar or coffee shop sporting one of these little devils: your basic trout sheathed in rabbit fur and presented to the credulous and gullible for their astonishment. The myth I use here is my own, though I may not be far off the mark, considering all the fish with huge carcinomas growing on their heads that have been dragged out of the Great Lakes in recent years.

Monstrous Reptiles and a Seven Foot Worm!

The *Sucuruju gigante* hails from the Amazon and may well be real. It is a snake reputed to have eyes the size of tea saucers and is many times longer than the longest of known snakes, the anaconda.

The *Lamighan Y Dwr,* or water leaper, is a fabulous winged snake you don't hear much of these days, but in the nineteenth century, this mystery beast was met with so regularly it was shot by farmers, who deemed it nothing more than vermin, of no greater significance than a rat or fox. It lived in the expanse of woodland surrounding Penllyne Castle in Glamorgan, Wales.

Rumours of the existence of a monitor-like lizard called the **Buru**, in a "lost valley" somewhere in the Himalyas, first began to reach the West in the 1940's. Several expeditions were mounted, which traced the tale to the Valley of the Apis Tanis, where this tale of the extinction of the species was related. No specimen or skeletal remains were ever collected, but the creature looks a lot like the monitor, with circular, serrated plates running like overlapping tiles down two sides of its bluntly-terminated tail. The creature was named by the locals for its plaintive cry.

Although it is an invertebrate, I put the Australian **Megascoliedes** in with the snakes and lizard on account of its enormous size. Imagine a seven foot earthworm — and the kind of fish you could catch with that! I did, and here's a hoary tale tale that'll make my nose as long as the worm!

Monstrous Jungle Vertebrates

Zaire appears to be home to a lot of nasty critters these days, everything from the monster virus Ebola Zaire to the saurian **Mokele Mbembe** (See **Why Were All The Werewolves Men?**, Thistledown Press, 1994). And Mokele baby ain't the only dino on the block! Also hailing from Lake Tele is the fearsome **Emela Ntouka,** a creature those who have seen it describe as a centrosaur or triceratops-like horned monster with a bad attitude.

From the jungles of the Cameroons, a country or two away, and Java, in the Pacific, come tales of a giant bat with feet that point backward, variously known as the **Ahool**, the **Olitau**, and the **Athol.** Is it real? Cryptozoologist Roy Mackal heard something in a cave he couldn't identify and others have been strafed by a creature with the wingspan of a condor. They describe the characteristic leathery wings and bat hands with long fingers supporting the skin of the wing.

But then maybe these tales are just a variant of the one about the **Kongamato**, a supposed surviving Pterosaur with viscious toothed beak, batlike-wings, and bad demeanor. It likes nothing better than to snack on men it picks up out of passing pirogues and is said to live in caves in high mountains overlooking jungle rivers in various places in Africa.

The **Nandi Bear** and **Mngwa** may be fearsome African bears, in a continent that knows of no bears, or fearsome cats or non-extinct prehistoric mammals. No one knows for sure. About all we know is that the first is a gourmand who prefers warm brains freshly hulled from the skulls of passing hominids, and that the latter would as soon rip anything in the vacinity to pieces. Some scientists have proposed a remnant of the supposed extinct Chalcotheridae clan for the first monster. We have only fur in the severed hand of many victims to speak of the other.

Hairy Bipedal Hominids

Readers will doubtless be familiar with the **Sasquatch** and the **Yeti**; less familiar are all the other hairy man beasts of the mountains, wild swamplands, forests, and jungles of the world. Virtually every country with a vast wilderness area can boast numerous sightings. Are these creatures new world apes? Are they renegade bands of primitive men? Neanderthalers? Or relatives of the massive, eight foot **Gigantopithecus**? The answer appears to be that Gigantopithecus, Neanderthal Man, and a diminutive yeti have all eluded science so far.

Bigfoot-like creatures include the **Missouri Monster**, or **Momo** for short; Florida's swamp-dweller, the **Skunk Ape**; Arkansas' **Fouke Monster**, and Texas' **Lake Worth Monster**.

In Central and South America, tales of huge new world apes get conflated with old world legends and myths, but there appear to be a least two, perhaps three creatures. One is a particularly nasty ape that looks like a five foot gibbon without a tail. Named by a oil geologist, Francois de Loys, whose crew came upon it in the jungles near Lake Maracaibo, Venezuela in the early part of this century, **De Loys**

Ape may or may not be the same creature as the feared ***Mono Grande,*** whose range extends into Guyana, where tales of another hairy biped, the ***Didi,*** abound. In Belize, the natives speak of a sneaky, more diminutive hairy dwarf known as ***Dwendi*** or the ***Dwende,*** but, again, whether this is a real creature or simply the hairy incarnation of the spirit of Dwende is uncertain. Brazilians fear an eight foot monster they call the ***Mapinguary*** and claim it likes to tear the tongues out of their cattle! Meanwhile, farther south in Argentina, around the foot of the *Imahhuaca* and throughout the state of Salta, the retiring, more diminutive ***Ucamar*** and ***Uco*** keep their distance from man.

And these are but a few hairy bipeds. China boasts its ***Wild Man*** of the thick forests of Shennongjia region of Hubei province; and the former USSR has its ***Alma*** of the Pamir mountain range, two ***Chuchunaa*** in Siberia (one hairy and humanoid; the other, almost certainly a stone age hominid who wears skins and uses primitive tools); the ***Yag-mort*** in the Urals; and the ***Kaptar*** or ***Almasty*** in the Caucasus. Tibet, of course, has the ***Abominable Snowman*** or ***Yeti,*** which just may be a surviving member of the Gigantopithecan line; but locals distinguish between it (the ***dzu-teh,*** a hairy giant) and a medium (man)-sized yeti, the ***meh-teh;*** and a smaller, three- to four-foot creature, the ***yeh-teh.*** Australia claims a ***Yowie*** and Sumatra and Java have their smaller ***Orang Pendek.***

Some scientists believe that many of the hairy man beasts in the five-foot range are surviving Neanderthalers, while it now seems likely that the larger, eight to twelve foot giants — ***Yeti, Bigfoot, Sasquatch,*** and their kith and kin — are either surviving Gigantopethicans originating in China or not very distant relatives of the great ape man.

Perhaps the ***Skrelling*** of the high Arctic is a surviving primitive — or was, until 20th century man made his acquaintance.

Just to complicate matters further, many cryptozoologists distinguish between the five-toed remote wilderness beasties which, in all likelihood, exist in this time and space, and so-called hairy bipedals from the Goblin Universe of UFO phenomena, which appear almost anywhere and as quickly vanish, after stealing a few chickens or being shot at. Their eyes appear to be orange or green and glow in the dark, and they frequently leave three-toed big footprints and are seen in areas where UFO flaps have simultaneously been reported. Some can imitate bird sounds or hoot; others just grunt or howl at the moon.

Fearsome Critters

But speaking of the Goblin Universe, man has never lacked imagination when he ran out of flora and fauna to catalogue, and whether his motive be publicity or pulling the wool over some greenhorn's eyes, he's come up with some pretty funny and far-fetched creature yarns over the years. From the backwoods of the Adirondacks and lumberjack camps the North American continent over come tales of the **Gillygaloo**, a bird that lays cubic, stackable and very portable eggs; the **Squonk**, a creature who hates his appearance so much he cries until he melts; the **Hoop Snake**, with venomous tail, capable of biting its tail and rolling hoop-like after its victims. Why they even say that his venom swells up scrub bush stalks to the size of tree trunks, and anyone foolish enough to build a house with that lumber will come upon a bird house when the swelling goes down! Then there is the rare fur-bearing trout (AKA the **Beazel**), already mentioned; plus too many other fantastic creatures to name — enough for your own book of fearsome critters, if you care to write one.

Incredible Occurences

A few of them intrigued me enough to write poems about. People really do spontaneously burst into flame, and it really doesn't have a lot to do with drinking too much alcohol, whatever the religious zealots and teetotallers say. And, yes, it occasionally does rain fish and frogs, and there isn't always a nearby typhoon which has whipped these poor creatures up into a vortex to make a same day delivery somewhere in Kansas. Weird goop does fall from the skies — goop the Welsh call **Pwdre Ser** ("rot from the stars") — and, while many folks would like to claim it is 747 lube goo or airline toilet flushings, the stuff has been taken to chemical labs, with inconclusive results. Is it nostoc — a blue green algae — or bird barf or industrial waste? Sometimes perhaps.

And what about the **Mad Gasser** hysteria that swept the town of Mattoon, Illinois in 1944? Was it a hoax based on an earlier hysteric episode that took place in Botetourt, Virgina in December 1933 and January 1934? Did someone really go around gassing people, or did an urban myth based on some night prowler incident get blown out of all proportion? I've had some fun speculating on a real motive.

Let's face it, **The Beast of Le Gevaudan** adds a lot of piquance to the werewolf myth, but it was probably a pack of starving wolves that accounted for those deaths. And, yes, things do go bump in the night and poltergeists and ghosts make frightening appearances. But who or what they are will have to wait for science to catch up with.

In the meantime, one thing is dead certain: **homo sapiens** is the worst monster of all, and he's capable of anything nasty!

If my tongue is firmly in my cheek in writing about these plausible or not-so-plausible creatures and anomalous events then, it is not quite so immobile or firmly lodged when it comes to consideration of my fellow hominids; hence, that dread denizen of the outer meninges, **The Lawyer**, who doesn't have quite so dainty a paw or so short a reach. But "Beware ... the Frumious Bandersnatch " and Homo Poeticus: they can be nasty buggers too.

ABOUT THE Artist

Gail Shepley (formerly Gail Mikla) is a graduate of The University of Lethbridge's Fine Arts program. She illustrated Richard's first collection of young adult verse, *Why Were All the Werewolves Men?* (Thistledown Press, 1994) and is adept in a variety of media. She currently paints, sculpts, illustrates, fabricates, teaches, and is raising a young daughter, Mary Rose, with her partner, musician/songwriter Jim O'Meara in Winnipeg, Manitoba. Jim and Gail are currently collaborating on a multimedia project entitled *Revelations.* Jim also has his chef's papers and makes sure no furry organisms occupy their refrigerator. While they don't exactly live high off the proverbial hog, the menu plan at their place beats Richard's hands down! there may be the odd unidentified fur-bearing organism in their refriger

ABOUT SASQUATCH

Readers may be interested to know that the collaborative efforts that have resulted in this book, its prequel and sequel, are ongoing. Recently, while playing with electricity in Richard's basement, a group of Rick's crazy hairy bipedal friends managed to create a living, breathing jazz/rock and poetry hybrid, Sasquatch. **Sasquatch** has arisen from the slab and ventured forth through the dry ice mists to perform at the **Calgary Young Writers Festival**, Edmonton's **The Word Is Out!** Book Festival, **The Park Place Mall** in Lethbridge, the town gazebo in Barons and elsewhere in Alberta. His personal hygiene and table manners have improved too! Anyone wishing to book **Sasquatch** for their favourite children's festival or party, or just wishing further information on the care and feeding of this delightful creature, should contact Richard. You can visit him at his website at http://www.pi-flora.com/pi/write/rs/default.htm, email him or fax or phone him, and he'll be happy to send you a press kit. Sasquatch will do workshops, performances, book signings, interviews and lunch!

ABOUT THE AUTHOR

Richard Stevenson (proper noun, sub-species homo poeticus) is a fully house-trained husband and father. By day, a full-time English and Creative Writing instructor for Lethbridge Community College; by night, a wide-eyed parent and poet, Richard is the author of ten published collections of poetry. His recent works include **From The Mouths of Angels** (winner of the 1994 Stephan G. Stephansson Award for Poetry), **Flying Coffins** (Ekstasis Editions, 1994), **Why Were All The Werewolves Men?** (Young adult verse, Thistledown Press, 1994), and **Wiser Pills** (HMS Books-on-disk, 1994). His children, Marika; and Adrian, cannot attest to Richard's culinary skills, but, so far, have not succumbed to anything he has revived from the slab in their kitchen. While there may be the odd unidentified fur-bearing organism in their refrigerator, nothing so far has amplified into a full-blown contagion or threatens their peaceful existence in Lethbridge, Alberta.

Printed and bound
in Boucherville, Quebec, Canada by
MARC VEILLEUX IMPRIMEUR INC.
in October, 1999